(Previous Page)

Mission San Juan Capistrano • 1926

This revealing wide-angled view shows a Mission San Juan Capistrano
battered by years of weathering and neglect, but enduring and saved by
loving efforts to restore it. Founded by Father Junipero Serra on
November 1, 1776 (after a false start the previous year at a different site),
it represented the first culture clash between the Indians
who had lived in what is now Orange County
for thousands of years and the Spanish newcomers,
who first arrived in 1769. The exterior stone wall,
in this photo recently, built with funds from the
family of oil tycoon E.L. Doheny,
replaced an old picket fence.
The front entrance is to the left.
The ruins of the Great Stone Church,
destroyed in an 1812 earthquake,
stand on the far right.

Photography: The First American Corporation

Orange County

Views of the

past & present

THE FIRST AMERICAN CORPORATION

FIRST EDITION 2003
PUBLISHED BY:
GEORGE ROSS JEZEK PHOTOGRAPHY & PUBLISHING
P.O. BOX 600253
SAN DIEGO, CA 92160
PHONE: (619) 582-7704
E-MAIL: GRJBOOKS@COX.NET

CONCEPT BY:
GEORGE ROSS JEZEK

PRODUCED BY:
GEORGE ROSS JEZEK

CONTEMPORARY PHOTOGRAPHY BY:
GEORGE ROSS JEZEK

CAPTIONS BY:
JOHN H. WESTCOTT

BLACK & WHITE PHOTOGRAPHS PROVIDED BY:
THE FIRST AMERICAN CORPORATION, HISTORICAL LIBRARY
UCLA DEPARTMENT OF GEOGRAPHY, AIR PHOTO ARCHIVES, PH: (310) 206-8188
ANAHEIM PUBLIC LIBRARY
IRVINE HISTORICAL SOCIETY

ALL COLOR PHOTOGRAPHS © GEORGE ROSS JEZEK

ISBN 0-9701036-2-X

GRAPHIC DESIGN BY:
MINK GRAPHIC DESIGN
PHONE: (714)-434-1405

PRINTED IN HONG KONG THROUGH CREATIVE PRINT MANAGEMENT, USA
E-MAIL: CPM2@EARTHLINK.NET

© GEORGE ROSS JEZEK

This book is dedicated to my father, George M. Jezek, who has been a constant source of inspiration throughout my personal and professional life. Without his unwavering encouragement, none of this work would be possible.

George Ross Jezek

Table of Contents

Introduction
BY JOHN H. WESTCOTT

Orange County is a land of great natural beauty, from the craggy cliffs of Dana Point to the rustic canyons of the Santa Ana Mountains. Man has added some beautiful sights of his own, including the ghostly ruins of the Great Stone Church at Mission San Juan Capistrano, and the graceful sandstone walls of the old Orange County Courthouse.

Indians saw the area's beauty more than 10,000 years ago. They settled in villages of thatched reeds and dined on acorns and abalone. Later, Spaniards also appreciated what they found here, building the mission and setting cattle loose on the golden hills.

In Orange County, Views of the Past and Present, we've sought to recapture the beauty that was Orange County, and show you the beauty that still endures, even after decades of tremendous change.

Photographer George Ross Jezek has a knack for picking up the subtle visual links between past and present. He delved deep into the archives of the First American Corporation and local historical societies for old photographs. He walked aging streets and clambered up dusty hillsides to match, as closely as possible, the angle of the historic photograph.

Getting just the right shot, in just the right light, took precedence over deadlines. Some photographers digitize over cloudy mornings. George will wait weeks or even months to get the perfect shot. What you see is nature's work, not Photoshop.

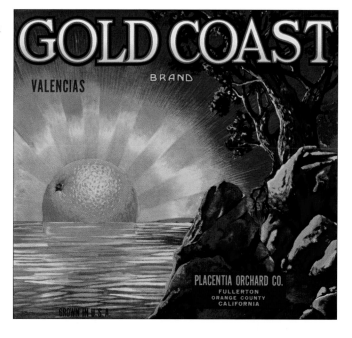

To write the captions, I dove back into the history I wrote about for the Orange County Register. What a rich history it is, from the Indians and the Spanish and Mexican ranchos, to the fascinating parade of newcomers that swelled into more than 3 million residents by the fall of 2003.

German families came to grow grapes. Polish artists fled Russian tyranny. Chinese railroad workers settled in small Chinatowns, and Japanese truck farmers concentrated around Gospel Swamp. Midwesterners were lured by promises of orange trees in their backyards. Then bold men broke away from Los Angeles County in 1889 to create the new county of Orange.

Soon the landscape was dominated by acres of sugar beets, lima beans and orange groves. Dozens of cities were born, fueled by railroad wars and real estate booms. Military bases sprang up out of nowhere, as the county helped fight World War II with airplanes and blimps. After the war, Orange County grew with incredible speed, growing faster than any other county in the United States.

Orange County has grown into an economic powerhouse and a symbol of the Southern Californian good life. With all of its amazing past and present, it is still a young county, with much history still to be written. It also has a lot of beauty that no doubt will be passed on to future generations.

They will look back and wonder, "Where did we come from?"

The city of San Clemente sprang from the ambitious dreams of Ole Hanson, the former mayor of Seattle, in the mid 1920s. His unique Spanish village by the sea was noteworthy for its elegant white stucco buildings, topped with red tile. For its first decade of existence, it was the only style permitted. The Hotel San Clemente was a grand way to visit the new city. The three-story hotel opened in 1927 on Avenida Del Mar. All 60 guest rooms were electrically equipped, quite unusual for the day. Rooms were advertised for $2 a night and up.
Chimes rang four times an hour from the hotel's roof.

Ole Hanson's dreams were given a rude awakening as the nation sank into the Great Depression in the early 1930s. Financially distressed homeowners were forced to sell and leave the city – Hanson among them. City leaders struggled to enforce the rules requiring only homes with white stucco and red tile, but in 1937 were forced to abandon them and allow other types of buildings. The Hotel San Clemente also ran into hard times, but survived. In the 1970s, it was refurbished and converted into a residence hotel. The old chimes were donated to the city in 1952, but a citizens committee raised funds to bring them back. Today, they still chime every hour, followed by a short song.

Oscar Easley played a major role in early San Clemente, grading the first streets in 1926 and serving on the first City Council. In 1929, he built the impressive two-story bank and office building on the left, in this shot looking toward the ocean. The building, at 101 South El Camino Real, was designed by architect Virgil Westbrook, who also created the San Clemente Beach Club. In the early years, the Easley building briefly housed San Clemente's city hall, a judicial office and the city jail. But its main tenant was the Bank of San Clemente, which became the Bank of Italy and later the Bank of America.

Over the years, the Easley Building has had some fascinating tenants. During World War II, scientists experimented with synthetic rubber on the second floor. Leo Fessenden's House of Music opened here in the late 1960s. A long list of doctors, dentists, architects, attorneys and real estate firms have called it home at one time or another, along with an antique store, an advertising company and other businesses. Today, its tenants include the San Clemente Historical Society and the San Clemente Chamber of Commerce. The building extends up the hillside, where the second floor is entered from Avenida de la Estrella.

This pier is the second built off San Clemente's coast. The city's founder, Ole Hanson, built the first, one of many public amenities he financed. He sold them to the city for $1 each, including the 1,200-foot Municipal Fishing and Pleasure Pier, built in 1927. The San Clemente Boat Club was built at the foot of the pier.
During Prohibition, rumrunners lifted booze up to the cafe at the end of the pier through a trap door. In 1939, huge waves swept away the café and all but 504 feet of the pier.
This pier, a bit longer at 1,277 feet, was built to replace it.

A ferocious storm in 1983 tore away the pier's midsection. It was rebuilt, but a surveying error left it with a humpbacked appearance until workers corrected it. The Fisherman's Restaurant, now at the foot of the pier, is a remodel of the old San Clemente Boat Club. Trains still rumble past at set intervals, chugging their way along the coastal route as they have since the city's early years.

THE FIRST AMERICAN CORPORATION

This prominent formation jutting from the southern coast of Orange County, just north of San Clemente, was called El Embarcadero during the Spanish mission days, and San Juan Point by early American immigrants. By the late 19th century, some called it "Dana's Point" for its association with Richard Henry Dana's seafaring classic, "Two Years Before the Mast."
It was far from the main cities of Orange County, but fishermen liked to troll its kelp-lined cove. Art Pobar built a tar-papered shack along the cliffs in 1911,
living off the ocean. He and a fisherman dug a road down the cliff, using only their hands. It later became Cove Road.

The cove remained mostly isolated and pristine for many years. The kelp beds were harvested for potash during the First World War. That unleashed the heavy waves, which began drawing surfers in the 1930s. They called it "Killer Dana." The surfing era ended with the construction of a breakwater and two marinas in the 1960s and 1970s. Now the beach is dominated by sunbathers, yachtsmen and others who just want a relaxing day under the sun. The brown buildings with the white roofs belong to the Ocean Institute, an educational and research facility operating here since 1977. Dana Point, which finally achieved cityhood in 1989, today has 35,000 residents.

THE FIRST AMERICAN CORPORATION

Dana Point inspired two attempts in the 1920s to build a city. A group of investors called the San Juan Point Corporation built an open-air pavilion in 1924, here dwarfed by the craggy cliffs, from boulders along the shore. It was named the Scenic Inn. Potential buyers trudged down rock-lined paths to dine on lobster, and an unidentified drink (This was in the middle of Prohibition). Even so, few buyers were persuaded. The first effort to build Dana Point failed.

A few years later, a second group of investors enclosed the Scenic Inn with glass to protect it from the elements. But that effort to build Dana Point also fell short, and it took decades before the city finally took shape. Dana Harbor today is overlooked by restaurants and lavish homes. Waves turned the Scenic Inn back into rubble long ago. Later, those boulders found their way into a restroom and barbeque pit that's still there today. You can see it just left of the parking lot.

THE FIRST AMERICAN CORPORATION

Dana Point was still largely undeveloped when the second attempt began to create a new coastal city here in 1927. This time the effort included Sidney Woodruff,
the man who helped build Hollywood and its famous sign. They built this pier in 1927 to take prospective buyers on fishing expeditions from Dana Cove.
Long before, during mission times, sailors tossed cattle hides off these cliffs, before carrying them off to their trading ships.
Woodruff hoped to build a modern community atop those same cliffs.

Dana Point is a far different place today, where thousands of people enjoy its rugged beauty and modern harbor. But Sidney Woodruff and his fellow investors couldn't entice enough buyers in 1927 to make his new community successful. The effort collapsed within a few years because of the Great Depression. Dana Point remained a tiny hamlet for decades. In the 1960s, the U.S. Army Corps of Engineers built a breakwater to tame the heavy waves. Workers moved 1.5 million tons of rock in a decade of construction ending in 1976, creating berths for more than 2,000 yachts.

Downtown San Juan Capistrano was already rich in history when this photo was taken, looking north down El Camino Real toward the mission. It is Orange County's oldest community, growing up around the mission founded in 1776. The Palm Café, on the right, was a popular local eatery for many years. The building was originally a schoolhouse in the 1870s. It was moved here in 1912, when it was converted into a restaurant. On the left is an adobe built by a Portuguese merchant named Manuel Garcia in the 1840s. Domingo Oyharzabal bought it in 1880, and remodeled it into the French Hotel and a general store.

The cars are modern and some buildings are gone, but downtown San Juan Capistrano has saved much of its past. El Camino Real has since been renamed Camino Capistrano. The Palm Café was renamed the Bird Café in the 1930s, and burned in 1937. The adobe is still owned by the Oyharzabal family. At 31861 Camino Capistrano, it is now occupied by an antique store, and is one of many structures from the Spanish and Mexican eras that San Juan Capistrano has preserved for future generations.

THE FIRST AMERICAN CORPORATION

The decaying walls of Mission San Juan Capistrano and the remains of its Great Stone Church haunt a historic landscape in this late 19th century photograph. It took nine years to build the church, which was perhaps the grandest building in North America when it was finished in 1806. It came tumbling down in a massive earthquake in 1812, killing 40 Juaneno Indians attending a sunrise service. It was never rebuilt. The Mexican government, which won independence from Spain in 1821, closed the mission in 1834. It became part of the United States after the Mexican War. President Abraham Lincoln gave the mission to the Catholic Church in 1865, shortly before his assassination.

The mission has mostly survived the ravages of time. Starting in 1895, several restoration efforts saved the walls from melting away completely. The latest restoration, still continuing, began in the 1990s. Scaffolding helps protect the walls. The nearby Mission Basilica San Juan Capistrano, completed nearby in 1986, is a larger version of the Great Stone Church. The mission remains the city's main tourist attraction, drawing close to a million visitors a year.

THE FIRST AMERICAN CORPORATION

Mission San Juan Capistrano stands mostly alone and neglected at the dawn of the 20th century. But it was like a mini city in the late 1700s, raising its own food and making clothing, soap and other necessary items, while tending thousands of cattle and sheep. Visiting trading ships valued the mission's cowhides – known as "California dollars."
On the right, the Great Stone Church's ruins lie next to a corridor along Father Serra's Chapel, and a corral where horses and other animals were kept.

Mission San Juan Capistrano is again bustling with activity, filled with tourists curious about the past. Artisans practice candle-making and other skills common two centuries ago in living history programs. Archaeologists dig for clues to the mission's history. The scaffolding shows where the walls of the Great Stone Church are being restored. The corral is gone, but Father Serra's Chapel is now the oldest active church in California.

The gently rolling landscape of Oso Canyon looks like much of the rest of the 52,000-acre Rancho Mission Viejo in the mid 1970s. Little was developed yet, just the early tracts of Mission Viejo, which saw its first residents in 1966. It was ranchland bought by Richard O'Neill in 1882, looking much as it did back in Spanish mission days.
But big changes were coming. Earthmovers began carving up Oso Canyon in October 1974 for the construction of Lake Mission Viejo.
The project was controversial at the time, performed in the middle of a lengthy statewide drought. The lake opened on June 3, 1977.

Lake Mission Viejo today is the centerpiece of the city of Mission Viejo, which incorporated in 1988. The 124-acre lake holds 1.2 billion gallons, and cost $11 million to create. A $1 million bypass-drainage system rerouted Oso Creek around the lake and prevents dirty urban runoff water from entering the lake. Mission Viejo has grown into a city of 100,000 people. Several new communities are growing on the rest of Rancho Mission Viejo, including Rancho Santa Margarita, Las Flores and Ladera Ranch. Planning is underway for development of the last 22,893-acre portion of the ranch, which will be a combination of housing and parkland.

THE FIRST AMERICAN CORPORATION

Nature carved these three arches into a large rock named Whale Island, inside a small Laguna Beach cove. Local Indians were the first to enjoy it, as evidenced by a small archaeological site on Whale Island. Local lore has it that early Spaniards called it "The Bay of the Three Little Windows." The first known white resident was a miner named Mr. McManus, who tried living off the land here in the 1870s. By the time this photo was taken, the same year the tiny artists' colony of Laguna Beach achieved cityhood, there were still only a handful of residents.

Multimillion-dollar homes now line the once lonely cliffs of Three Arch Bay. Starting in about 1930, Dick Rowland built roads and planted trees and worked to improve and grow the community for more than two decades. Cecil B. DeMille supposedly once considered building a castle on top of Whale Island. Many early silent movies were shot here, including *Captain Blood* with Errol Flynn in 1935. Three Arch Bay voted to call itself South Laguna in 1934, but the small cove still goes by Three Arch Bay. The three arches are still there, of course, a natural gateway between the sandy beach and the tide pools.

Before Pacific Coast Highway ran its ribbons of asphalt through Laguna Beach in the mid 1920s, only a dirt road cut through a rustic landscape, mostly free of traffic.
The skyline contained only a scattering of homes. A deep depression in the road was covered with a narrow wooden bridge.
Sleepy Hollow was a small valley in a corner of the tiny village of Laguna Beach.

Sleepy Hollow is anything but sleepy today. Urban growth left little trace of the small valley. Douglas Fairbanks and spouse Mary Pickford helped dedicate a stretch of Pacific Coast Highway running through Laguna Beach in 1926. Sleepy Hollow was filled with dirt, and the bridge replaced with concrete and asphalt. Sleepy Hollow was near where Cleo Street is today.

Laguna Beach was distant from other cities in the early years, but people were drawn to its scenic views and the pristine beaches, especially Main Beach. Some built summer beach cottages close to the water. Such noted artists as Frank Cuprien and Norman St. Clair came to depict the scenery on canvas.

Most came just to enjoy the sunny beaches. Those who did had to observe the social mores of the time.

In 1929, a man was arrested for indecent exposure; that is, for wearing bathing trunks, not the full-body bathing suit expected of both men and women.

Most of the small cottages have been replaced by large, multi-million-dollar homes and elegant restaurants, built ever closer to the water. Laguna's Main Beach has evolved into a year-round playground.

The opening of Pacific Coast Highway through Laguna Beach in 1926 made the city much more accessible from the more populous areas of Orange and Los Angeles counties. A growing number of tourists, including movie stars, began to enjoy its beaches, restaurants and hotels. One was the White House Café, to the left, which first began serving meals in 1918. Thomas Bird bought it in the late 1930s, and soon was urging patrons to "Let the Birds Feed You."

The White House Café, at 330 South Coast Highway, today is the only local business on the highway still in its original building. The magnificent three-story structure on the right is the Hotel Laguna, which in 1930 replaced the ramshackle Yoch Hotel, barely visible in the earlier photograph. Lauren Bacall, Lana Turner, Humphrey Bogart and other stars frequented the hotel, at 345 South Coast Highway, and gave it a Hollywood allure. Today, this stretch of Pacific Coast Highway teems with tourists in the summertime.

Laguna Beach's earliest American residents included homesteaders who planted groves of eucalyptus trees to prove their land claims in the 1870s. The eucalyptus forest became so thick that wagons and buggies couldn't get through to the beach, so some trees were cut down to make a path. It was called Forest Avenue, and it was the entrance to Laguna Beach in the early years. By the 1920s, the corner of Forest and Park, which connects at Pacific Coast Highway, became famous for The Gate.
The sign greeted visitors passing by Rankin's drug store with the words, "This gate hangs well and hinders none.
Refresh and rest, then travel on."

As the years went by, businesses changed, buildings were torn down and replaced, and traffic swelled along Pacific Coast Highway. But The Gate still remains. Forest Avenue is still a gateway to the heart of Laguna Beach, just an easy walk from the Main Beach, with fine dining or an ice cream cone from the parlor where Rankin's drug store once stood.

George Brown and Joe Farrell opened the Cabrillo Ballroom, left, in 1926, and it soon became a popular fixture on Laguna's Main Beach. Lovers of jazz and dancing made the Cabrillo the best-loved dance hall between Long Beach and San Diego. The Joseph Sanford Orchestra and others inspired patrons to partake of its 7,500-square-foot dance floor. On some Saturday nights, you could see Judy Garland and Mickey Rooney enjoying the sounds – or even Mickey filling in on drums.

THE FIRST AMERICAN CORPORATION

The Cabrillo's heyday was over by 1940, when it was converted into a bowling alley and pool hall. The building was sold in 1958 and later torn down. Laguna's Main Beach today is enjoyed by sunbathers, surfers and basketball players, among others. Nearby, thousands of visitors come for the art festivals, Pageant of the Masters or just a day at the beach.

THE FIRST AMERICAN CORPORATION

Crescent Bay is one of several rugged and beautiful coves along the coast of Laguna Beach, which were largely untouched by man for thousands of years. It was still sparsely populated when this photograph was taken. The cove is about a quarter mile in width. A rocky formation on the west side came to be called Seal Rock, because of the seals and sea lions that took long sunbaths there.

A small community gradually grew around Crescent Bay through the years. Homeowners now share the beach with big crowds in the summer, including volleyball players, skim-boarders, body surfers, and the scuba divers who explore its beautiful reefs. Crescent Bay has kept much of its rugged beauty despite the area's growth and popularity, and is one of the few places in Orange County where you can still find sea lions.

This dramatic coastline just north of Laguna Beach dates back to mission days, when the Spanish called it El Morro (bluff) for the dramatic dome of rock that looms over it.
The land later became part of the Irvine Ranch. Campers began pitching tents on the beach in the 1920s, coming in greater numbers after this stretch of
Pacific Coast Highway opened in 1926. The year before, Robert Windolph secured a lease from the Irvine Company and
created Tyron's Camp on Morro Cove.

The tents were replaced by recreational vehicles by the 1940s. The domed rock was named Abalone Point for the delicacies found in tidal pools underneath. Tyron's Camp became El Morro Camp, then El Morro Trailer Park after the Peyton family bought the lease in 1954. Later, trailer spots became mobile homes. El Morro found itself part of the 2,791-acre Crystal Cove State Park when the state bought the land from the Irvine Company in 1979. The state and El Morro residents have tussled over the mobile home park's future, which may be resolved by the time its lease expires at the end of 2004.

THE FIRST AMERICAN CORPORATION

In 1904, George E. Hart bought 706 acres in the southerly corner of the Irvine Ranch. It was called Rocky Point at the time, but Hart soon had a new name for it: Corona del Mar, Spanish for "Crown of the Sea." He built roads, homes and Hotel Del Mar, the three-story building overlooking the bluff on the left. The pier that leads to a small shack was a stopping place for launches that carried passengers across Newport Harbor to the Balboa Peninsula. The larger buildings and pier in the foreground were built later.
Aside from a bumpy dirt road, the early ferry service was the only way to get to or from Corona del Mar.

Several private piers now jut from this tiny cove. Long ago, the extension of the Pacific Electric Railroad that Hart had anticipated never materialized, and Corona del Mar remained relatively isolated until the Pacific Coast Highway was completed in the mid 1920s. That's when Corona del Mar finally began to develop into the desirable community it is today – too late for Hart, who had sold out a decade earlier. Many of Corona del Mar's older homes built on the bluffs have been torn down in recent years to make way for larger ones.

Corona del Mar's rocky shore became home to the Balboa Palisades Club in 1925, built by Pasadenans as a private beach club. Beach clubs sprang up all along the Southern California coast in the 1920s as get-aways for upwardly mobile inlanders. Like all crazes, this one eventually fizzled. This club shut its doors after just three years. The building was soon bought by the California Institute of Technology (Caltech) and named for the electricity mogul who supplied the funds: William G. Kerckhoff. The house on the upper right, built about 1919, was the beach home of W.J. Hole, who helped to found the city of La Habra.

Beek charged five cents to get across the bay. The ferries worked continuously in the summer when there was enough business, and every 30 minutes the rest of the year. In 1921, the first cars were carried across on a barge, pushed by the "Fat Fairy". The ferries and their names changed over the years – the "Joker", "Square Deal", "Commodore" and "Islander" were some of them – but the ferry service remained constant and reliable. The Beek family still runs the business.

Newport Beach and its harbor had begun to take shape by the early 1920s, but its waters were still too treacherous for most boats. Newport Harbor had been carved by an early version of the Santa Ana River many thousands of years ago. The sandspit that became the Balboa Peninsula was created in the mid 1800s. Balboa Island had been dredged from the harbor bottom by 1913. The many mudflats and sandbars made navigation hazardous. The west jetty had been built, but was not enough to prevent a huge sandbar from clogging much of the bay's entrance. One ship was stranded for five years before it became dislodged.

Newport Harbor today is one of the most popular recreational boating harbors in the United States. Soon after the earlier photograph was taken, workers dredged up silt from the shallow bay to create Lido Isle. But it took another decade before enough money was raised to thoroughly dredge the bay and build jetties on both sides of the harbor entrance. The $1.8 million project came from a combination of federal and county funds. The harbor was dedicated May 23, 1936. President Franklin Roosevelt pressed a telegraph key on his White House desk to signal a Coast Guard cutter outside the harbor. The cutter fired a cannon that began a celebratory yacht parade.

This small ranch house, built in 1868, was one of the first wooden buildings erected between Anaheim and San Diego. James Irvine, who left famine-stricken Ireland for America in the 1840s, built it on the ranch he and three partners bought from Don Jose Andres Sepulveda in 1864. Sepulveda's Rancho San Joaquin was the first piece of a 125,000-acre land empire bought by the partnership. Irvine built this two-story home as a place to conduct business when traveling from San Francisco. In 1874, the partnership hired Charles French as ranch superintendent, and he moved into the house. Irvine bought out his partners in 1876 and became sole owner of the ranch.

Today, only the cooking wing of the ranch house survives, lying on the edge of the Rancho San Joaquin Golf Course. In the early years, loneliness was a big problem for Charles French. Fleas were so numerous he flooded the floors. Later, Irvine's brother-in-law lived in the house briefly. The cooking wing was added, which can be seen in the first photograph, and the house became the cattle foreman's home for many years. The Irvine family built a larger house in the northern part of the ranch, which became the family's home after the 1906 San Francisco earthquake. The old house fell into neglect, and was torn down in 1961. But the old cooking wing became the Irvine Historical Society's museum in 1980.

Irvine Country Store • circa 1925

The Irvine Country Store, seen from the side in the center of the photograph, was run by Kate Munger. A determined young woman, she repeatedly petitioned James Irvine II to run the store and won, despite his prejudice against women running businesses. The store opened in 1912 in the tiny Irvine Ranch town of Myford. The building faced Central Avenue and also contained the town's post office. Behind it and to the back, the Irvine Hotel was built in 1913 for migrant workers.
In between the two buildings, a small gas station opened in 1915.

This historic corner of the Irvine Ranch is now a dirt lot, awaiting its future. The hotel originally faced Laguna Road, but that road was closed and rerouted after a wealthy car dealer died in a railroad accident at the nearby Santa Fe crossing. The hotel was turned 180 degrees to face Burt Lane (now Burt Road). The Munger family ran the Irvine Country Store for many years before the lease was sold. It was still selling pickled pigs' feet and brass washboards into the 1980s. But the ranch was changing. Central Avenue became Sand Canyon Avenue, Myford became East Irvine, and a large swath of the ranch incorporated into the city of Irvine in 1971. The store and the hotel were moved across Sand Canyon Avenue in 1986, and became part of Old Town Irvine shopping center.

As the 19th century drew to a close, the Irvine Ranch shifted from sheep grazing to barley, lima beans and other crops. As the need for storage grew, this warehouse was built in 1890, followed five years later by a mirror image of it just behind it. Each 350-foot-long warehouse could hold up to 200,000 sacks of lima beans or barley, each weighing 100 pounds. The warehouses stood next to the tiny town of Myford, named after the son of James Irvine II, just north of the Santa Fe railroad tracks. By the 1920s, the Irvine Ranch was the lima bean capital of the world. The warehouses hummed 24 hours a day at harvest time.

A concrete silo building, which replaced the old warehouse, is now a hotel. By the 1940s, many farmers were mechanizing their operations. James Irvine II resisted the change, but after he died in 1947, the 1890 warehouse was demolished. A bed of sand was laid to cushion the new building from railroad vibrations. The new bulk silo warehouse, completed in 1949, had 32 silos that could hold a total of 16 million pounds of beans and barley. Fifteen men did the work of 100. But soon, farms began giving way to housing tracts. Irvine became a city in 1971, and the silo was closed. In the 1980s, the silos were remodeled into rooms for La Quinta Hotel. Restaurants and other businesses occupy the old warehouse building behind it.

This 45-foot double arch next to the pier once greeted visitors to downtown Huntington Beach. It spanned Ocean Boulevard (later Pacific Coast Highway) where Main Street ended at the Pacific Electric train depot. Drivers traveling Pacific Coast Highway could see the words "Huntington Beach" in 14-inch-high enamel letters starting in May 1929. The building on the right is Rexall Drugs.

© GEORGE ROSS JEZEK

Redevelopment in the 1980s reshaped much of downtown Huntington Beach. Jack's Surfboards occupied the old Rexall building for years. Now the surf shop is one of several tenants in the new Oceanview Promenade. The steel arches, part of an effort to bring more tourists to Huntington Beach, ruled over the intersection through the 1930s. They were often decorated for the holidays, as were some of the tall wooden oil derricks along the highway. The arches finally came down in the early 1940s. One reason was the constant upkeep they needed because of the salty air.

Anyone driving down Pacific Coast Highway in Huntington Beach after 1920 was treated to the sight of a forest of oil derricks. They still dominated the city's skyline when this photo was taken looking northeast from the pier. The large building on the beach was the Saltwater Plunge, built in 1911. The plunge's heated waters were just the ticket for both tourists and the local crowd who didn't want to brave the ocean's cold and sometimes treacherous surf.

The beach has changed dramatically over the years. The plunge was covered, and was gone by the 1960s. Oil derricks continued to loom over the coastal landscape until recent decades. At the time, they were a terrible fire hazard. The city fire chief ordered the removal of many derricks in the 1950s to create a six-block-long firebreak. Today, smaller pumps still dot Huntington Beach, but the city's coastal area has been almost completely cleared of its oil legacy.

THE FIRST AMERICAN CORPORATION

When oil wells began gushing thousands of barrels a day from beneath Huntington Beach in 1920, oil fever seized the city, and still hasn't let go of it completely. Thousands of oil derricks standing 120 feet high – like these looming over the ocean near 17th Street – dominated the city's geography, economy and even its politics.
Some tiny lots considered so worthless in 1914 that they were given away for the price of a set of encyclopedias,
suddenly became worth thousands of dollars when oil was discovered under them.

The oil derricks are gone from this corner of Huntington Beach, but they dominated the city's skyline for decades. As late as the 1950s, Huntington Beach residents often begged oilmen to drill wells in their backyards. But as the years went by the oil boom finally began to wane, and people started valuing the city more for its neighborhoods, schools and beaches than for its black gold. The tall derricks were outlawed as unsightly, and removed or replaced by smaller pumps by the early 1970s.
Oil is still pumped in parts of Huntington Beach, and it remains an important part of both the city's past and present.

The tiny town of Harper changed its name to Costa Mesa in 1920, just in time for a post World War I boom. This busy corner of Newport Boulevard at 18th Street, looking north, was witness to much of the growth. The city was blossoming so fast that its new grammar school, opened a year after this picture was taken, was overcrowded after just five months. The Costa Mesa Bank occupied the newly completed two-story building, built of hollow tile with a brick front. It stood just south of TeWinkle's Hardware and north of the Wayside Market. The market was torn down and replaced by a larger building and a different market within a few years.

The scene is different but some buildings are the same. The Great Depression closed the Costa Mesa Bank in 1932, and the city went without a bank for years. The building was later occupied by a dry goods store. In recent decades, the second story was removed. Roma Designed Italian Furniture now occupies the building. Much of Newport Boulevard, long a gateway to Newport Beach, was split by the extension of the Costa Mesa Freeway in the 1990s. The north and south lanes rejoin just north of this stretch. Costa Mesa, which now has 103,000 residents, is a shopping and entertainment mecca, boasting South Coast Plaza, the Orange County Fairgrounds and the Orange County Performing Arts Center.

The Kushino Brothers store, where one could buy Japanese goods in early Fountain Valley, stood at the crossroads of Bushard and Talbert avenues. Then the small town was called Talbert.
It stood in the middle of Gospel Swamp, a boggy corner of west Orange County, named for the traveling preachers who used to pitch tents here for large evangelical revivals.
It was difficult soil. Farmers banded together to drain it before any large-scale farming could be done on it for sugar beets and lima beans.
It was also a remarkable multi-cultural mix, with Americans, Japanese and Mexicans all working the land.

Bushard and Talbert is a very different place today, with senior housing rising not far from where the Kushino Brothers store stood. The store burned down a few years after the first photo was taken. The town grew slowly over the years. Japanese farmers were taken away to internment camps during World War II, but many returned afterward. When Fountain Valley became a city in 1957, Jim Kanno was elected the first Japanese-American mayor in the United States. Today, the city is still a strong mix of ethnicities, with large Hispanic and Asian populations. Fountain Valley, which takes its name from the many artesian wells once found in the area, has about 55,000 residents.

The swampy soil that once dominated western Orange County made farmers search hard for crops that could grow there. Perhaps the most successful was the sugar beet. The Santa Ana Cooperative Sugar Company built this sugar beet processing factory on Dyer Road in 1912, after James Irvine gave a 33-acre site and much of the funding. More than 2 million bricks went into the factory's construction. It was the last of six sugar factories built in Orange County. The road was named after Ebenezer Dyer, who built California's first sugar beet factory in San Francisco in 1879. By the time this photo was taken, the factory had been bought by the Holly Sugar Company.

There's none left today, but during World War I, Orange County's sugar beet factories produced a quarter of the nation's sugar supply. At its peak, the Dyer plant processed beets from 50,000 acres planted on the Irvine Ranch. The Holly Sugar Company bought the Santa Ana plant in 1917. Like many of the county's big crops, the sugar beet fell victim to pests and development. Holly processed the last beets from the county's soil in 1973, and by then was importing them mostly from the Imperial and San Joaquin valleys. Birtcher Pacific bought the factory's remaining 23 acres in 1983. The Embassy Suites hotel was built on part of the site. The factory would have been on the hotel's left.

The commercial center of Santa Ana dominates this view of Fourth Street looking west at Bush. The tallest building then, middle right, was the First National Bank. On the far right is French's Opera House, created by entrepreneur Charles E. French for the city's cultural edification in 1890. It was renamed the Grand Opera House seven years later. For 33 years, it hosted many plays, and even some boxing matches – but not a single opera. The steam engine tracks running down the center were replaced by the Pacific Electric's trolley lines a year after the photograph was taken.

The scene is far different today, much of it shrouded by trees. The Bank of Tustin survived several crises over the years that closed other banks, including the national Panic of 1893. But the bank finally shut its doors in 1902. It reopened as the First National Bank of Tustin in 1911. By the 1930s, the turret had been removed. Tustin's library occupied a back room after the 1933 earthquake. The First National Bank eventually merged with First Western Bank. It closed for good in 1962, and the building was demolished. The land became a parking lot for Tustin Hardware, now an antique shop.

Tustin was still a small town when this photo was taken, with only a handful of businesses. Most were here, on the south side of Main Street between El Camino Real and C Street. The family of Columbus Tustin, the town founder who died in 1883, lived upstairs in the two-story building, over the family's meat market. The building with the pillars was Charles O. Artz General Merchandise. A burglar broke into the Artz store in the 1920s, only to die of cyanide poisoning because the family was fumigating it.

The old Artz store, which dates back to 1914, has had several owners. It now features the popular Rutabegorz Restaurant, which moved into the building in 1978, and still amuses customers with its neo-hippie menu. Next to it, the meat market and Tustin home were replaced by a new building just a few years after the first photo was taken. Today, Gary's & Co., Cass Hare Hall and stores selling draperies and shoes occupy the other 1914 building, to the east.

THE FIRST AMERICAN CORPORATION

Sheep graze near the two huge hangars of the Santa Ana Naval Air Station, south of Tustin. James Irvine II had to give up some of his prized lima bean fields when the U.S. Navy came calling with an urgent need for military bases at the beginning of World War II. A conventional aircraft base was built at El Toro. But these hangars, at $2 million each, were decidedly unconventional, housing blimps. Dirigibles helped patrol the California coast from Del Mar to Santa Barbara in search of Japanese submarines. No subs were ever sighted. By 1950, the hangars were empty, the land leased back to Irvine for grazing sheep.

The old Bank of Orange building was torn down in 1927 and replaced by the present building the next year. The two banks merged, and became the First National Bank of Orange. Wells Fargo bought the building in 1977, and shares it and the building on the right with Starbucks. To the right, wood siding now hides the brick of the 1899 bank building, which has undergone several major remodelings. Today an accounting firm occupies it. The old bank vault and safe are still inside.

When Orange Union High School began in 1903, students went to class in an empty store on Glassell Avenue. The school's 83 students and four teachers soon found a more permanent home on Shaffer Street near Glassell. The center building was the first one completed, in 1904. It became known as the Academic Building, and is flanked here by the high school's Science and Commercial buildings. About five years after this photograph was taken, the Academic Building was moved 300 feet from Glassell and given a quarter turn. The move made room for Memorial Hall, a 99-seat auditorium, completed in 1923.

THE FIRST AMERICAN CORPORATION

Memorial Hall (in the middle) contained an auditorium, administrative offices and the school's library. In 1947, the building was declared seismically unsafe. The school district decided to erect a new school elsewhere, and sold the old buildings to Chapman College, a private Los Angeles institution not bound by the strict seismic codes for public buildings. Chapman, named for Fullerton benefactor Charles C. Chapman, moved into the buildings in 1954. The old Academic Building became Wilkenson Hall. The small liberal arts college was renamed Chapman University in 1991. Today it has 4,500 students and a growing academic reputation.

St. Joseph Hospital was born out of the horrors of the 1919 flu epidemic. The Sisters of St. Joseph devoted itself to providing better medical care, and was invited to Orange County in 1922 by Archbishop Cantwell. It bought the Burnham estate on Batavia Street in the city of Orange and began building a sanctuary and hospital. When St. Joseph Hospital opened on September 18, 1929, with 120 beds, it was the region's most modern hospital.

The original St. Joseph Hospital building now sits behind a more modern facility. In 1964, the sisters built this new 290-bed hospital. The same year, Children's Hospital of Orange County opened next door. Today, St. Joseph Hospital is a 448-bed facility, and is still not-for-profit and Catholic-run. The original building, with its graceful towers in the background, is still in use today, mostly housing laboratories.

THE FIRST AMERICAN CORPORATION

Three friends of Madam Helena Modjeska pose in front of her magnificent canyon home, designed by famed architect Stanford White in 1888. Modjeska was one of America's finest actresses of the late 19th century. Modjeska, her husband Karol Bozenta Chlapowski, future Nobel laureate Henryk Sienkiewicz and other artists left their native Poland in 1876 to escape Russia's heavy-fisted rule. They started a small farming colony near Anaheim, but the farm was a flop. She learned English and began acting again. She bought this property deep in the foothills of the Santa Ana Mountains from James Pleasants, the bearded man on the right. Her home, named Arden from the forest in Shakespeare's "As You Like It," was built around Pleasants' old cottage, which stands in the middle.

Madam Modjeska's home is now a county historical park. She lived here until 1906, when she grew weary of exhausting railroad tours of America's theaters. She moved first to Tustin, then to a cottage on Bay Island in Newport Beach. Her death in 1909 prompted headlines around the world. Her home became the Modjeska Inn for several years. The Walker family bought it in 1923. For a while, the Walkers ran a small exotic zoo featuring a brown bear. The family sold the home and the grounds to the county in 1986, and it was preserved as a historical park. Both the canyon and a nearby mountain peak are named for Modjeska, who brought a little acting magic to the county before the days of movies and television.

Seal Beach began as Bay City, just another quiet beach town. In 1915, Philip Stanton rebuilt a 1906 pier and lengthened it to 1,865 feet, the longest south of San Francisco. That year, the city partied all night long when it incorporated under the new name of Seal Beach. The parties continued as Stanton added the Jewel City Café at the foot of the pier and a roller coaster nearby. Fifty-two scintillator lights were installed at the end of the pier, so powerful that it was said to illuminate the ocean with multicolored lights for 50 miles. Seal Beach became a "sin city" popular for gambling and drinking – both illegal at the time.

The wild party days are gone and Seal Beach is again a quiet beach town. After leaving his mark on the city, Philip Stanton went on to an impressive political career, becoming speaker of the state Assembly. The pier remained a major city landmark even as the café, roller coaster and scintillator lights all disappeared by the mid 1930s. The pier was badly battered in the storms of 1939 and 1983, but was repaired each time. Seal Beach is no longer the "Coney Island of the Pacific" that Philip Stanton envisioned, but it is home to more than 25,000 residents, and a popular spot for surfing and sunbathing. Ruby's Jewel Café now occupies the end of the pier.

A stroll down Main Street during Seal Beach's wild days in the 1920s probably would have included a stop at the Seal Beach Pharmacy, seen here looking north on Main Street not far from the pier. Old-timers who shuffled in on their way to the beach recall when the interior had a dirt floor.

Today, the building, at 111 Main St., is occupied by Clancy's cocktail lounge. As the city of Seal Beach evolved over the years, so did this building. It became a bar, the first called Mott's, and then Mamie's. In 1957, the Meier family bought the building and named it Clancy's.

Bicycles share the road with an early automobile on Almond Street, now Westminster Boulevard. The city began as a Presbyterian temperance colony, founded by the Rev. Lemuel Webber in 1870. It was named for the Westminster Assembly of 1643, which laid out the basic tenets of the Presbyterian faith. Farmers refused to grow grapes for years because of its association with alcohol. The temperance days were mostly gone by the time this photograph was taken. Looking west from Olive Street, the largest building on the right is the Oddfellows Hall, built in 1900. In front of it is Orville Day's store. J.F. Patterson, the city's first postmaster, owned a feed store in the double-peaked building on the left.

Nearly all of the buildings from the original photo are gone. Westminster, which incorporated in 1957 with only 10,755 residents, began growing at a manic pace after World War II, quadrupling in population in the 1960s. Like Garden Grove, the city received a large influx of Vietnamese refugees in the 1980s. Today the city has 86,000 residents.

On the left is the First National Bank, at the northwest corner of Euclid Avenue and Ocean Boulevard. It was the financial center of Garden Grove, beginning as the Bank of Garden Grove in 1909. Alonzo G. Cook bought 160 acres south of Anaheim in 1874, and planted an experimental garden before naming the new town he created Garden Grove.
Later, Allan Knapp was called the "Chili King" for developing the dried chili industry in the city, and for a while the city considered itself in the "egg capital of the world" for its egg and poultry industry.

The Anaheim Town Center shopping center now occupies this greatly changed scene. The Kraemer building is the only structure from the original picture still standing. Most of the buildings endured well into the 1970s. The Hotel Valencia had already seen its better days when a kitchen fire burned it down in 1977. A massive redevelopment of downtown Anaheim tore down SQR, the Fox Theater and many other buildings within a couple years. Center Street was renamed Lincoln Avenue, and this stretch of it was rerouted to the north.

Anaheim • Disneyland • Aerial • 1955

The brand-new amusement park of Disneyland, just a few days after the grand opening on July 17, 1955, is surrounded by a still-rural panorama of Anaheim. The scene, looking northeast, includes many of the orange groves that still dominated the city's landscape in the mid 1950s. The nationally televised opening was something of a disaster. Many rides broke down, women's high heels sank into Main Street's freshly poured asphalt, and drinking fountains didn't work yet because of a plumber's strike. But nothing could dampen America's enthusiasm for Disneyland. It took just seven weeks to reach 1 million visitors. Disneyland, borrowing ideas from Knott's Berry Farm, showed that amusement parks didn't have to be seedy and dirty.

106

Disneyland has grown and changed considerably since the early days, adding dozens of rides, shops, restaurants and other attractions. To the right of Disneyland is a newer Disney theme park, California Adventures, which opened in 2001. Together, the two amusement parks drew more than 17 million visitors in 2002. Anaheim, which started as a grape-growing colony of German immigrants in 1857, also has grown, to more than 310,000 residents. The city's mighty entertainment empire also includes major league baseball's Anaheim Angels, and hockey's Mighty Ducks.

THE FIRST AMERICAN CORPORATION

Long before the Knott's Berry Farm we know today, motorists stop at the Buena Park berry stand of Walter and Cordelia Knott. Travelers bought berries and Cordelia's jellies, jams and berry pies. The Knotts struggled for years, scratching out a living in the Mojave Desert and San Luis Obispo County before they rented 20 acres here in 1920 with Walter's cousin Jim Preston. The beach traffic on Grand Avenue (today's Beach Boulevard) often stopped at this berry stand and helped the couple to make ends meet through the lean years. But with the Great Depression of the early 1930s, the Knotts would need something else to get them through: the boysenberry.

The original berry stand was located near the ticket booths at today's entrance to Knott's Berry Farm. The stand has moved several times since the early days and is now in the parks ghost town. Most of Grand Avenue was renamed Beach Boulevard and rerouted to the east of Knott's Berry Farm, but this stretch alongside the park entrance still has the old name. In the early years, Knott specialized in various berries, but was elated to discover a new variety developed by Rudolf Boysen, Anaheim's parks director. Boysen had no interest in doing anything with his discovery, a cross between a blackberry, a red raspberry and a loganberry. Knott named it after Boysen, and the large, flavorful fruit helped saved the Knotts from losing their farm during the Great Depression.

THE FIRST AMERICAN CORPORATION

The cluster of buildings that grew into today's Knott's Berry Farm gathers on the west side of Grand Avenue. It all centered on the original Chicken Dinner Restaurant, on the right, built in 1934. Cordelia wanted to offer homemade chicken dinners to the many travelers stopping by for jellies and preserves, so Walter built this small "tearoom."
On the first day Cordelia served her first eight chicken dinners on her wedding china, for 65 cents each. The lines kept growing longer even as
Walter Knott added room after room. He asked a bank for a $10,000 loan, but restaurants were considered too risky.
Even after the banker reconsidered, the Knotts financed it themselves, completing the expansion in 1937.

The Chapman Building, at 110 East Wilshire Avenue, remains an imposing historical presence in Fullerton's downtown. In the early years, Ferber's Department Store was the building's main tenant, occupying the basement, first floor, mezzanine and second floor. Glass bricks embedded into the sidewalk filtered light into Ferber's underground dressing rooms. The building began a long decline in the 1950s. It was completely restored in the 1980s, and refurbished again in 1997.

During Fullerton's building boom of the early 1920s, city leaders took the unusual step of funding a grand new hotel through public subscriptions, giving citizens part ownership in the venture. The result was the California Hotel, built on the northwest corner of Wilshire and Spadra Road (later renamed Harbor Boulevard). Charles C. Chapman, the city's first mayor, headed the Fullerton Community Hotel Company, and contributed $25,000 of his own money. Local architects Frank Benchley and Eugene Durfee created a U-shaped, three-story building with an open courtyard. The California Hotel cost $136,000, and was dedicated on January 15, 1923.

The city took great pride in its new hotel, which boasted stores, 22 apartments and 55 hotel rooms. The Fullerton News Tribune regularly published the names of visitors staying there. In 1965, the aging hotel found new life as Villa Del Sol, a shopping center with an elegant restaurants and offices. A one-story addition closed off the front courtyard, tile roofs and second story balconies were added, and turrets were removed from the towers. The building was extensively rehabilitated in 1995.

This building began as the Alician Court Theatre in 1925, built by C. Stanley Chapman, the son of Fullerton's first mayor. He named it in honor of his wife Alice. Made of brick and concrete, the theater became a combination vaudeville and silent movie house. The architects, Meyer and Holler, Inc., also designed the Grauman's (now Mann's) Chinese Theater in Hollywood. It was known as the Alician Court Theatre only briefly. After several name changes, it became the Fox Fullerton Theatre in 1930, the year after it became the first theater in Orange County to feature "talking" pictures.

The Fox Fullerton Theatre now lies empty, hoping for a rebirth. In its early years, the theater had six canvas murals on the inside walls, but they were painted over in a 1955 remodeling. The Mary Louise Tea Rooms once were on the north side of the theater, and a series of retail shops occupied the south side over the years. The theater closed in 1987, and hasn't opened since. A citizens group is collecting funds and hopes to restore it.

The Placentia Mutual Orange Growers packinghouse stands as a proud symbol of the city's prominent role in the county's orange industry. The orange steered Placentia's destiny, as well as Orange County's. It began in 1880, when Richard Hall Gilman planted five acres of Valencia oranges, a new and untested variety imported from Spain. It did well and within a few decades much of the county was blanketed by Valencia groves. Packinghouses dotted the county, half a dozen in Placentia alone.

Some growers banded together in associations for bargaining strength, including the Placentia Mutual Orange Growers in 1910.

They moved into this modern building on the northwest corner of Melrose and Crowther avenues in 1921.

The rose-colored brick building, which today is an office building, churned out boxes of oranges for the association for more than half a century. The brands it shipped included Albion, Altissimo, Cambria, Caledonia, Marvel and Shamrock. As late as 1950, Placentia probably had more orange trees than its 1,682 residents. After World War II, Orange County began to replace more and more of its orange groves with housing tracts and shopping centers. Soon, most of the fruit shipped from the Melrose and Crowther packinghouse came from San Diego and Ventura counties, as more and more orange groves were torn out for housing tracts. The Placentia Mutual Orange Growers packinghouse finally closed in the mid 1970s.

THE FIRST AMERICAN CORPORATION

Oil derricks festoon the hills north of Brea, off Brea Canyon Road. Early Indians, Spaniards, Mexicans and Americans used the tar and oil oozing from the hillsides for waterproofing, lubrication and other uses. But as the 20th century and the age of the automobile arrived, so did the demand for huge quantities of oil. New oil towns like Petrolia, Olinda and Randolph (later Brea) sprang up to house the oil workers pumping thousands of barrels of crude oil out of the ground.

Oil was discovered elsewhere in North Orange County, dominating the economies of La Habra, Fullerton, Placentia and Yorba Linda for decades.

There's still a few oil derricks on these hillsides, but the oil boom years are over. The hillsides once made the area one of the top oil producers in the state. Oil crews here set a world record in 1927 for the deepest well up to then, 8,046 feet. As Brea has grown into a full-grown city after World War II, the vast oil field has slowed its production and housing development is creeping up the foothills. Today, the city has about 38,000 residents.

Brea was still a bustling young oil town when this shot was taken, looking north on Pomona Avenue from Ash Street. The town's original name was Randolph. But Brea - Spanish for the tar that oozed from the foothills - proved more appropriate. The first of many oil wells was drilled in 1898. The Brea Hotel, middle right, was completed in 1912. The white building at the top of the street is the Brea Grammar School, which was built for $66,000 and opened in 1917.

Pomona Avenue is now Brea Boulevard, redeveloped almost beyond recognition starting in the 1990s. The Brea Hotel, also called the McCarty Building, went by several other names over the years: Kinsler, Ozark, and then Sherman in the late 1930s. Under the latter name, it was spruced up with new awnings and stucco. It continued as a hotel for many years until it was finally torn down. The Brea Grammar School and its Greek revival architecture went through many changes through the years, but endures today as Brea Junior High.

THE FIRST AMERICAN CORPORATION

Frank Nixon built this simple wood-frame farmhouse next to his small Yorba Linda lemon grove in 1912. There, on January 9, 1913, Richard Milhous Nixon, probably the most prominent person to emerge from Orange County, was born on a brass bed. He was a studious child who liked to take swims in the nearby irrigation channel when his father wasn't looking. It was a harsh land for growing lemons, so the Nixons moved to Whittier. Later, Richard made the debate team at Fullerton Union High School, and prepared his first law cases in a La Habra office building. By 1959, when a plaque went on the house noting Nixon's service as vice president, it was a home for maintenance workers at nearby Nixon Elementary School.